YouTube

The Secret to Building an Audience and Creating a Massive Passive Income

Anthony Smith

Table of Contents

Introduction

Congratulations on purchasing your personal copy of YouTube: The Secret to Building an Audience and Creating a Massive Passive Income. Thank you for doing so.

The following chapters will discuss some of the many ways you can use your personal videos to earn money. People spend billions of hours watching YouTube videos each and every month. In addition to this fact, YouTube is one of the most popular websites on earth apart from Facebook and Google. For anyone who wishes to learn how to earn income passively online, passing up this opportunity would be a big mistake!

You will discover how important the opportunities presented by YouTube are. It's a great medium for traffic and branding. There have already been many successful entrepreneurs who have done just that. In this book, you will learn about what you have to do to make quality videos, promote your channel, and have a successful passive income source from YouTube.

The final chapter will explore a few more ideas you can incorporate into your plan for earning money through your videos so that you have every corner covered and are equipped to give this your best shot.

There are plenty of books on this subject on the market, thanks again for choosing this one! Every effort was made to ensure it is full of as much useful information as possible. Please enjoy!

Chapter 1
What to Know about Earning Money
with Videos

In order to successfully use YouTube to sell, you have to have a few things first. Let's look into some physical products you must have in order to make this work, and then we can get into some digital bases you must have covered and ideas for marketing.

Products you must have to Start Earning on YouTube:

Obviously, YouTube relies on videos, so you will have to have a setup for recording videos, first and foremost. Contrary to how it may sound, this need not be elaborate or even expensive. It's perfectly possible to make professional looking videos and spend less than $1000 on your setup. Here is what your setup needs to include:

- **A Camera for Recording:** This is an obvious piece of equipment you will need. Choose a product that will shoot a minimum of 720p, or better yet, 1080p if possible. If you are going to use a webcam, Logitech is a good brand while being quite affordable. For those who would rather use a digital camera, Canon is recommended.

- **A Microphone:** A quality microphone has a large impact on the way your videos turn out. You can opt for a USB style microphone if you need to do voiceovers. If you are working with a limited budget, you can find one for less than $100. Eventually, when you earn more money, you can always upgrade to something nicer if you wish to do so.

- **The right Lighting:** Using overhead lighting that many rooms already have will cast a shadow on your videos which isn't as appealing for YouTube. You can invest in an affordable, simple setup for lighting that will give your videos a far more professional feel to them.

- **A Camera Tripod:** If you do end up using a digital camera, a tripod is a great investment. A tripod helps to make the video more stable, which isn't necessary when you're using a webcam. These can be found, typically, for less than $100, but that does depend on what type of camera you're using.

- **A Background:** Your videos can have some extra character if you have a good background. Using a sheet of large, seamless paper can work, but for more serious video makers, a background made specifically for photography will be needed, along with some fabric to go with it.

- **Software for Editing Videos:** If you're just making simple videos, extensive software for editing probably won't be necessary. A simple movie making program (like iMovie for Mac or Movie Maker for a Windows computer) should be enough. All of these products together will give you a higher chance of success.

Do you have a Website yet?

A landing page or website is a must for this, also. Trying to earn money with YouTube without this is going to be a much slower process since YouTube is mostly useful for the traffic it can drive to your other sites. So, how do you benefit from this once you have your own store or website?

When you create videos, people need to have a link to click that will bring them to either your product page, store, or blog. You might also want to link to your Facebook or Twitter account depending on the strategy you're using for marketing. In each video, use a different dedicated linked page. For example, if you have a video about how to properly pack for a trip, this can serve as a way for people to find the products you talked about in your video. Sure, this takes more work, but it leads to more results, too.

Focusing on Adding Real Value:

This sounds strange, but in order to effectively sell anything using YouTube, you have to get rid of the expectations you have of selling. Rather, you should try to help those who view your videos by offering value and advice. Sales tactics nearly never actually work in this format, but entertainment value and good advice do. People don't like the feeling that someone is trying to sell them something, so this cannot be your primary focus if you hope to have any success in this area. As soon as you've met the requirements above, you can start making videos.

Chapter 2
Creating Engaging Video Content on YouTube

For years, video clicks were what counted in the ranking system of YouTube, that's about to change. Instead, it will matter more how long videos hold the attention of viewers. Catchy titles or pictures as the video thumbnail are no longer enough and it will soon be mandatory to have videos that have real value to them in order to gain loyal subscribers and, eventually, customers. So, how do you stay relevant in the midst of this change? Here are some tips for doing that.

Tips for Holding your Audience's Attention:

- **Who is your Audience?** This is a question you must know the answer to. You ideally should have the ability to say who your audience is, including their age range, hobbies, and interests. Which benefits are they searching for and what words are going to hold their attention?

- **Get to the Point:** Ensure that your views find out within the first few seconds why they must continue to watch your video. Tell and show them what they will gain from watching.

- **Be Energetic:** Those who show that they have energy and passion for what they're doing on their videos will be much more successful at keeping the attention of their viewers than those who are dull and monotonous.

- **Be a Risk-Taker:** As soon as you've figured out who is watching your videos, trust your intuition about them and don't be afraid to take risks. You can't just follow the path that someone else has set and expect to have great success. Instead, think like an entrepreneur.

- **Have a Script and Plan for your Content:** Your first goal in this area should be to decide what your YouTube channel is going to deliver to its audience. After that, you can start to plan out the video structure you'll be using. What do you love to create? What skills need to be developed in order to do this? Don't just try to copy whatever happens to be trending on existing channels. You will have success when you follow what you actually care about.

  Having a script increases the likelihood that your video performance will go better. Not only does it help you keep your video content organized and efficient, but it helps you stay on topic as you talk. No one likes to watch a video of someone rambling on and forgetting what they were saying every two minutes. Plan for this and make your videos well-structured.

- **Making Quality Videos:** This is an obvious one, but creating great content is a must for keeping your viewers around. Ensuring that you keep it quality throughout the whole video, and not just at the beginning, is a must for making sure that your viewers stay with you the whole time. Videos that work best will be either informative or entertaining, but the absolute best is both. This is standard knowledge for any type of marketing content, but specifically, videos should both entertain and inform to be successful.

Be Honest and Genuine:

People respond best to truth and honesty. Just consider the obnoxious car salesman that everyone thinks is fake and mildly annoying. You don't want to be just another salesman! Instead, show your true ideas and self in your videos, including your own sense of humor, and even some of your personal emotion. This genuine touch is what people tend to appreciate when it comes to their favorite video creators. Being fake will not get you far for long.

- **Make them Want to Return:** Make sure that your videos will both capture the audience's attention, but keep them coming back. One method for doing this is uploading videos that have a more viral type of entertainment content, but also uploading videos that you hope people will come back to again and again. For those who don't like being on film, screencasts are an option. However you decide to do it, make a policy that you only publish content that is informative and adds value to the life of those who watch it.

- **Building Incentive**: Give viewers a reason to want to come back to your YouTube page by hinting at what you will talk about in future videos or the next upload you create. This builds a sense of anticipation and will leave them thinking about what your next video will be about. This is a basic marketing strategy that all successful content creators already know about, so make sure you take advantage of this simple but effective tool and strategy. Let's look at what else you can do to increase the engagement of your viewers and video content you upload.

Having a High Upload Frequency:

People subscribe to your video channel because they like your work and hope to see more of it. Subscribers will not appreciate a channel that doesn't put out new videos on a regular basis. Particularly in this modern day, viewers will be hoping for more entertainment regularly, so you have to be ready to keep up with this demand. You have to utilize consistency if you want to develop a relationship that lasts with your audience. Try to release each video you make in a recurring, timely, and structured way, on a weekly basis if you can. Let your viewers know that they can count on you to bring them what they like; your great content, of course!

Creating a Schedule for your Videos:

If you can't publish weekly, try for bi-weekly or monthly. Stay with your publishing schedule and try not to veer off course with it. Viewers like being able to expect when they will see a new video. This allows them to anticipate the content you will deliver and appreciate it even more when they do have access to it. This will help you build a loyal following that returns to your channel time and time again and eventually helps you build your passive income from YouTube.

Chapter 3
How to get More YouTube Subscribers

Content on YouTube is in the lead for marketing content in the year 2017. It's free, and while other companies try to compete with the game of video marketing, such as Twitter or Facebook, they have had nowhere near the amount of success that YouTube has had. For anyone who already has a channel on YouTube, the question of whether you can earn money from it is a logical one. To do this, though, you first have to have a lot of subscribers. How do you do this?

How to Increase your Subscribers on YouTube:

YouTube has more than a billion new visitors each and every month, meaning that there is a huge audience potential with every single video uploaded. Whether it's comedy material or makeup tutorials, YouTube is the first choice platform for viewing video content. Plenty of new stars are rising on YouTube, so it's certainly the right platform to use for people hoping to get publicity and marketing. You can use it to broaden your reach to your followers by making the connection more personal. The chance a blogger has to use this medium to their advantage and gain high levels of traffic from this site is pretty high, but first requires that you have more subscribers.

- **Cover the Details in your Script:** When you make up a script for your videos, make sure that you are as detailed as possible. Include the precise words you will use, along with the actions you'll cover in your video, along with the major points to talk about, and specific calls for your audience members to take action on. You should also know who your audience is and craft a script that is based on what they understand. Are they from America or not? Do they know about technology? Are they looking for entertainment value, or something more informative and detailed? All of these questions will help you think about who they are and use the right words to tell them what they want to know.

- **Optimizing Video Titles:** Standing out in the crowd is a must for being successful in this area, and giving your content unusual names is one way to do this. That will have people coming to see your channel or videos out of curiosity. But getting plenty of views is about more than just that.

Using SEO for Greater YouTube Success:

In order to get the most views possible, you will have to take a look at marketing and SEO. SEO stands for search engine optimization, meaning that you have a chance to show up when people search for content related to the subject you're covering on your YouTube channel. The first step of doing this is optimizing the titles you have so that they extend and reach further. Here are some basic tips for doing that:

- **Using Keywords in your Video Titles:** This used to have a bigger impact than it does now, but with video it still has a decent effect. You can use AdWords on Google to find out what it is that people are looking for online, and then try to make videos that blend together low competition and high searches.

- **Have a Shorter Title:** To have success with this, your title shouldn't be too long. Try to aim for a title that is 50 characters or less, an engaging description, and is descriptive enough, offering a preview to the content of the video. If you need more help with writing relevant, catchy, and optimized video titles, do some extra research on this topic, or simply experiment to find out what works best.

- **Using Customizations for your Channel:** If your plan is to get your audience to trust what you are selling on your channel, you need to use the options for customization that come with it. Making sure that you look professional will ensure that your viewers trust and respect what you have to say. If you have a blog already that has some followers, use similar elements of branding for your channel on YouTube so that you will be recognized on both.

This can involve using channel art that distinguishes your brand and you as a person. This is offered on YouTube for an affordable price. You could also look into having a header that is custom made and has some elements of design from the existing blog you have. Take advantage of the custom URL and channel bio sections to make this even more personalized and customized. For those who are interested, provide a blog link in your video's description.

- **Using Thumbnails:** Most creators on YouTube agree that making a custom thumbnail for their videos is better than allowing the randomly generated thumbnails. You can use relevant images and annotations as custom choices and this will improve the number of clicks you get. Adding a small annotation to your custom thumbnail will let your audience know what the video is going to cover.

- **Using a Trailer for your Channel:** YouTube gives video creators the chance to use trailers that will allow you to play a video automatically when your channel opens. The trailer you choose should be worked on carefully and improved constantly in order to keep your viewers interested and engaged. You have to use this moment to capture your viewers' attention in just seconds. Your trailer should be between half a minute and one minute, and you should give reasons why your viewers should stay on your channel and what you can offer to them.

This is obviously easier for those who are naturally comfortable with a camera. Try to give a quick, engaging, informative introduction based on a script you decided upon beforehand. You can read through the channel reports for your YouTube account, looking at the rates of viewer retention, in order to see if you are losing potential viewers with a lengthy or boring trailer. Then keep making adjustments until you have a perfect trailer.

- **Using Calls to Action:** Annotations for calling your audience to action are those little popups that come up while they are watching the video. These can lead to a higher number of subscribers by including them to click the popup while they watch your video. Many video creators on YouTube have noticed increased subscriptions to their channel when they added these. You can put in a link that encourages audience members to subscribe, or you can use a graphic. If you do this in a way that isn't annoying or obnoxious, your subscriptions will grow as a result. However, if you do this in an annoying way, you might actually lose potential subscribers.

- **Using the Correct Tools:** There is no shortage of useful tools in this area, from video creation tools to video promotion tools. Using the correct resources will aid you in growing your organic video views. When you have organic video views, you have access to a higher number of potential audience subscribers.

- **Allow People to Discover you:** YouTube gives users the choice to click a link and get sent to your website. So if you already have a website, do this as soon as possible. There is absolutely no reason not to take advantage of this option if you can. Any effort you dedicate to bringing video views to your channel can be taken advantage of any time you direct viewers to your webpage. In addition, this will make your channel a verified, authentic source for your personal brand.

In your YouTube page channel settings, you can add your blog URL or website to the channel.

You could also add your URL or website to the description of your YouTube channel. You can also add a subscribe option button on your webpage or blog to bring more subscribers to your channel.

- **Make your Videos Shorter**: Your videos shouldn't be any longer than five minutes. Even though YouTube houses many in-depth, detailed reviews and longer videos, the videos that have the highest conversion rates are shorter than five minutes. Most YouTube videos are around four and a half minutes, so this is a good range to shoot for as a beginner on the site. Stick with this until you have a reliable following for your account, and then you can mix it up and experiment with different lengths later on. It can be hard to keep videos entertaining, informative, simple, and also short, but it will be well worth the effort you put in.

- **Intros and Outros**: The intros and outros you use for YouTube will aid you in branding your name and also will help your videos have a higher entertainment value. This will give your videos a professional feel and can be used as a sort of opening theme, similar to a show that people come back to and enjoy the familiarity of. In addition to this, an appealing intro ensures your audience is more involved with your videos.

- **Be a Ruthless Editor**: In order to get the best of your content out on the web, you have to make a lot of it, and edit it ruthlessly. Most creative geniuses make a lot more content than they actually show, and what we see is their best work. This should apply to your YouTube videos too. Edit them fearlessly to ensure that you are only publishing your absolute best videos. When you try to force yourself to publish on a strict schedule without taking the time to make the videos good, your brand will be hurt down the road. Make plenty of recordings for your final cut, but only publish the best. If you aren't sure about a specific take, you can always take multiple shots. If you're using Windows, Adobe Premier is a great program for editing your videos.

- **Optimizing Descriptions in your Videos**: Returning to the SEO (search engine optimization) side of making YouTube content, you should never neglect the descriptions of your videos. Your video descriptions will allow your content to be easily discovered in a search engine while also giving your potential audience members a sneak preview of what your content discusses. However, this shouldn't be overdone.

Putting a really detailed description in your video won't make any sense because the first few sentences are the only parts that are displayed when someone loads the video. Like your video's title, the keyword should be used in the video description but not overdone. You can't outsmart search engines by entering the keyword 20 times. In fact, that will likely just hurt your odds of getting displayed on search engines. Instead, make it authentic and natural.

- **Use Meta Tags for your Videos**: You can put Google's Keyword Planner to good use by finding relevant ideas to use for keywords in your videos, then adding them to your content and videos. This will allow you to be easier to discover on both YouTube and Google searches. If you overdo this, it's not going to help (and will actually do the opposite), but adding in some well-placed and researched words will help your rankings a lot.

  Keep in mind that if you have a low view count on your videos, it doesn't always mean your content isn't good. It might just mean that it isn't easy to discover for viewers. Metadata plays a bit role with allowing your content to be more easily displayed to those who are searching. Look at some videos that are well-converting and look at the meta tags they have on them in order to get an idea of what works. However, don't simply copy/paste these tags because that won't work.

- **Think about How you End them**: No matter what your video content is about, you should always end videos on a high note. Similar to the very last bit of dialogue before a play ends, videos should end in a way that is memorable and positive. Ask the viewers watching to subscribe and like your video if they enjoyed it, and then ask them to visit your blog our website. Keep in mind that if you don't ask for anything, you won't get anything. End all of your content with a confident flourish, allowing viewers to know you appreciate them. End videos in a positive way, smiling and leaving your audience eager to see more content from you.

- **Think about Collaboration**: You can collaborate with other video creators on YouTube. In fact, this has turned into quite a common act among video makers. Why is that? Because when you collaborate, everyone benefits from it. Your audience benefits, the people involved in the collaboration benefit, and so do you. Creativity is all about being constructive, and viewing other video creators as just your competition doesn't help. Instead, celebrate the success of others and see how you can join together to improve each other's success.

  Look for successful video creators in your field and see if you can collaborate to make an interesting project. And always remember to look for what you can add to their channel as well. This will let you connect with new audience members that you may have never reached before, and the person you collaborate with will also have access to new viewers. The audience will appreciate the new value and extra content, as well. As you can see, this is an advantage for all parties involved.

- **Make sure you Interact with Viewers:** The art of social media relies on interaction and connection with people who share your common goals and ideas. This means that the amount you care directly influences your success. When the people viewing your content can tell you actually care for them as people, they will return the favor. No one wants to be involved with someone who doesn't care about them, even when they are just YouTube subscribers. Make an effort to interact with your viewers, paying attention to the requests they give you in comments.

You might get some anger or backlash in comments, but don't allow that to distract you from paying attention to your loyal listeners and viewers. When your viewers take the time to comment on your videos, make an effort to respond to what they're saying. That will build some trust between you and your audience, leading them to respect you for taking the time to connect. This is how you build a loyal fan base.

- **Do Challenges and Offer Prizes**: Who doesn't like to receive prizes or complete challenges? After you build up a loyal fan base, you can offer them some kind of compensation for staying true to your channel. A contest or prize giveaway can help you to lure in new viewers and reward those who have stood by your channel. You can give away T-shirts, a tech gadget, or a free hosting subscription. The possibilities are endless. No matter what you choose to give away, your viewers will appreciate receiving something free and will likely share this with their friends.

Not only does this give you a chance for free promotion, but possible viral promotion for your YouTube channel. For huge giveaways, some hosts on YouTube require that their audience members must subscribe to each of their social media platforms before they can enter the giveaway, which is a great approach. The prize items should be relevant to the niche your videos are about, but it's okay even if they are not.

- **Promoting Across Platforms is a Must**: In our modern social media age, being active and present across different platforms of social media is a must for succeeding and growing any type of online audience. When you are attempting to create a brand for yourself, you have to be discoverable. This means being active on more than one platform for social media. Try putting up profiles on Google Plus, Twitter, and Facebook. However, you can go further and put up Instagram and SnapChat accounts too. You can give Google and Facebook ads a try to in order to give yourself further promotion.

  When you are visible throughout various platforms online, you are making yourself far more visible. Make sure that you are being aggressive about securing your first followers, which will, in turn, motivate you to create better content. You can't just build a great website and expect your customers to show up right away. Use every resource you can to build up your brand. You can also share your channel with interested friends, but try not to hassle or pester them.

- **Keep on Trying**: Experimenting and changing your methods until you find what works is the best approach anyone can take. Remember that there is never one single path to success and that what works for others might not always work best for your personal pursuits. Find what works for your brand and channel. This could include switching up the thumbnails, backgrounds, camera angles, and other techniques given to you in this chapter. Pay attention to the way your audience changes according to these changes, and always stay true to what your brand is about.

Making something memorable and valuable on YouTube will require lots of perseverance, time, effort, and dedication from you. However, if you stick with it and stay patient, it can work for you. These are only guidelines to get you started. Don't be afraid to think outside the box and come up with your own methods!

Chapter 4
Selling on YouTube and Affiliate Marketing

In order to start to make money from YouTube, you first have to get comfortable with making your very own, personal videos, of course. For some, this can sound easier than it really is, especially for those who are shy or nervous to be on camera. But once you get a quality setup for recording and a few ideas going, you will start to have fun with putting content on YouTube. The type of video content you will make will depend on what you're trying to sell, but let's get started with a few specific ideas you can test out on your YouTube channel.

Ideas for making your YouTube Video Channel more Interesting:

- **Have a Question and Answer Segment:** Your audience members and customers will probably have some questions to ask you about the product you are selling, whether it's before you sell or afterward. You can make a list of any questions they have and answer them on your channel. This is like a FAQ for your channel and will save you time on answering the same questions time and time again.

- **Show Behind the Process Scenes:** People are often interested to see the process behind manufacturing, particularly in processes involving branding. When you create a product of your own, you should show how the process of manufacturing goes, which assures your customers of what your brand is all about. It also allows them to see the quality of what you make and see the culture behind your business.

- **Topical Video Content:** FAQ type videos and behind the process videos are great, but they are limited in the potential they have to reach and entertain your audience. Content focused on topical industry information has the potential to reach a bigger viewer base, however. These videos should help your audience members gain an understanding of issues and finding solutions to them. In addition, it can focus on entertainment, knowledge, and facts. If you, for instance, sell accessories related to traveling, you could put out videos about packing efficiently, or items you might need while taking long trips. But when you want to have viral videos, try to make informative, short ones like Buzzfeed videos.

- **Involve Product User Stories:** How do real customers make use of what you sell? Interviewing your previous customers and telling their personal stories is a good idea for YouTube video content. Contact your past customers to ask them if you can use their stories for your channel. Many of them will agree wholeheartedly (particularly if their blog or business can be promoted in your video). Interview them at their place or have them come to your video studio. This works very well for branding purposes and general testimonial sharing.

- **Sharing Others' Reviews:** Finally, your channel doesn't need to be limited to only your personal videos. It should ideally include other people's content too, particularly review videos done by other YouTube video creators. These reviews can be found by searching the name of your brand or product on the website. Then ask the video blogger for permission to feature their review video on your account. The majority of bloggers will be glad for the exposure.

How do you Gain YouTube Traffic?

The next thing you need to do once the videos are made is bring video traffic either to your landing page or website. Thankfully, YouTube gives users a few different ways to let people interact with YouTube content and videos. Below, we will discuss a few of those ways.

- **Annotations for Similar Content:** We already briefly discussed annotations in the previous chapter, but make sure that you use them to link to any videos you have on your channel that are related or similar, so users stay on your YouTube page.

- **Cards for Interaction:** Interactive cards are a new addition to the marketing tools on YouTube. These elements can be placed in your videos to perform functions such as showing websites, products, other video content, or even to raise money from within the video. In order to make use of this, read up on the help section on Google to figure out what card you can use and how.

More for Marketing and Growing your Audience:

As soon as your videos are done and uploaded, you need to keep working on promotion for your YouTube channel. Depending on the skills for marketing you already have, this could be either the hardest or easiest part of selling for you. Employ these tactics any time to get a head start, even if you are a complete beginner with marketing.

- **Get Creative with Answering Questions:** As mentioned before, engaging with your audience is a must for having a successful channel. Of course, YouTube commenters aren't always the most thoughtful or polite, but engaging with the ones that are will help your brand's success. Instead of just answering the questions of your commenters, though, try looking up videos about similar subjects created by other YouTube users. If you sell work out equipment, for example, look up related videos and leave comment responses on there. This increases your visibility.

  Please remember to never aggressively push your products. This is a strategy that plenty of people use and it nearly never works because people don't like being pressured to buy things. Instead, leave helpful hints to commenters that they can find out more about the subject by going to your videos. Your priority at this stage must always be to be offering value and help, and the money will come later on.

- **Making Relevant Titles and Descriptions:** YouTube is a wildly successful search engine (the second biggest one on the internet). In addition to being its own successful site, it dominates searches on Google too, these days. Videos are displayed in more than half of Google's search results and most of those are YouTube videos. We've already covered a bit on SEO before, but let's look at some other tips you can use to improve yours on your channel. Make sure that your video keywords already have some existing results on Google. The keywords should have at least two results already online.

When you make your video title, make sure you use those keywords and ensure that the name of your video file also has those same keywords in it. For instance, if the name of your video is "Packing on a Trip," the title and name of the file could be "packing-trip.mp4" and "Packing on a Trip, a Detailed Guide" in addition to that. Your video description should have a length of at least 200 words to describe your video and have a positive impact on the content's SEO.

- **Think Bigger**: We talked a bit about adding your content to your other social media platforms and profiles, such as Google and Facebook. But you can take this a step further by messaging Twitter accounts and Facebook pages that are in related niches and request that they share your content. A lot of pages like that are searching for good content that they can share with their viewers and subscribers. For content of yours that is big or newsworthy, get a hold of news outlets or blogs like Huffington Post and more and ask them to share your content. You can also link to your video in community forum areas like Reddit.

- **Promotion on YouTube**: Even though you should focus on promoting your content on other sites, you should of course dedicate plenty of time to promoting your videos on YouTube itself, as well. This involves creating playlists that are optimized for SEO, so that they will show up in the pane of related videos and add to your existing views. Make a separate area requesting that people become channel subscribers for your content and put this segment into each video that you make, pointing at the subscription button with annotations.

If you do all of the steps above, you will notice that selling on YouTube, and gaining viewers, doesn't have to be a difficult chore. It should be viewed as a process that will develop over the long term, not a scheme to become a millionaire overnight. Rather, invest your time in this process and grow your audience authentically with the attitude that you want to help others and add value to the internet. Whichever future sales you do end up making later on will naturally come this way, after you have built a trustworthy and respected brand for yourself.

Using Affiliate Marketing for Earning on YouTube:

Another method people can use to earn money on YouTube, get a passive income, and eventually gain financial independence and freedom is through YouTube monetization using affiliate marketing. Affiliate marketing is when you supply links to other people's products and bring them sales through your audience members. Not only can you earn money from ad impressions left on your videos, but by putting affiliate marketing links in the video descriptions. Typically, these earn even more than video ads, plus it has the benefit of benefiting many different people. Stick with these tips if you want to be successful in this area:

- **Stick with What you Know:** If you are trying to be as general as possible in your videos in order to gain a bigger audience, cut out this strategy now. Instead, stick with what you already know! People want to hear from those who have personal experience with what they are talking about, not someone who is just trying to sell them something. If you're an artist, talk about paint supplies, if you're a fitness expert, link to books on nutrition or exercise clothes and equipment.

- **Be Relevant:** For this to work well, you do have to make sure you plan right. For example, only link to relevant products that have to do with the subject you're discussing in the video. Otherwise, it will just come across as confusing. Doing this also gives you the benefit of an audience who is more likely to be interested in what the link is selling, follow it, and buy something.

- **Get People to View:** As soon as you have some affiliate links in your video descriptions, you should just work on getting more views, which you are probably already working on! In order to be even more successful in this, get some of your content uploaded and then work on becoming a partner on YouTube. This gives you an added chance to have higher ranked videos. If you don't know what kind of videos you should make, there are plenty of articles online giving out free ideas for this.

Some affiliate marketing opportunities will pay you for every click you get on their product link, while others require that the people actually buy something before you get any earnings from it. The best part is that, either way, you are earning income completely passively just by having the link there on your video description. Seek out products relevant to your niche and find what works for you to benefit from this method of earning on YouTube.

Chapter 5
Using AdSense on YouTube

YouTube is a great stream for revenue, and this is true for many different companies and businesses. However, incoming money is usually small when you only have a small audience. Sure, you can monetize your video content without using AdSense. However, the properties linked with Google will allow you the extra advantage of having everything you need in one place (a single control panel). AdSense is a great resource and tool, especially for people who already know how to use it. Linking up your YouTube and AdSense accounts is very simple, but it might require some waiting time for Google to process and approve your application.

How can you Link your Existing AdSense and YouTube Accounts?

When you already have an approved account with AdSense, and you have a YouTube account that qualifies to be monetized, you will find the process of linking them together painless and very simple. Here are the steps:

- Go to the page for your channel settings in your YouTube account, then access the monetization option. This should bring you to a section on How to get Paid.

- Find the Association page on AdSense and go through the steps it gives you for going to AdSense. Continue and use your Google account to login. It must be the one that you are using with your YouTube channel.

- Click "Accept" for the association with AdSense and let your internet browser get redirected back to the YouTube page.

This is all you have to do. By now, Google will need to go through and process the request you just entered, which might take a couple of days to go through. As soon as this is activated, you can manage ads on YouTube using AdSense from Google, taking advantage of the control and analytics that come along with it. The steps for monetizing your videos when you don't yet have an account with AdSense are basically the same as this.

You need to go to your settings in the channel and visit monetization settings. But then once you get redirected over to AdSense, you have to create an account on AdSense. This does take a little longer than the steps listed above, but it's pretty simple to figure out. You can also follow these instructions to edit any settings you need in this area.

Restrictions for Monetization:

There are, of course, restrictions to this, as well. YouTube doesn't let people monetize any content. Your videos only qualify if you are the owner of all rights to what the video includes, on a worldwide and commercial level. What this means is that your content can't have content that you don't own selling rights to or completely own yourself. Your videos have to abide by the terms of service and YouTube's community guidelines. Although this seems easy enough, there are a few things that might ruin your video's eligibility. Let's look at some of these flags that mean you cannot upload the video:

- Any video with background music that is copyrighted, live performances of copyrighted information, or specific sound files that are commercial.

- If your video has logos from any businesses that aren't yours, this is a restriction that means you don't own full rights to the video content. This also applies to videos with software that is not your own within them.

- Media property, video game, or movie footage that you don't own the rights to also disqualifies you from using that video for monetization.

All of this can be a bit complicated, particularly when it comes to the modern day copyright laws. For instance, you can't use songs for your video content, even if you did by the song to listen to yourself. You first have to get a commercial license if you wish to use it beyond your own personal listening purposes, which can't always be done at all.

Image Complications and Rules to Adhere to:

Another restriction you should think about is stock images. You can of course use images within your video content, but you need to own the rights to that image every time. This means images that you yourself have created or that your business owns, like your business logo. Any images that you have bought to use commercially from a site that hosts stock images are fine, as well, but you can't just pull any photo you find on Google images and use it in your videos.

Sure, there are countless YouTube videos that have game feeds, movie footage, or audio that the video content creator doesn't own, and sometimes these are monetized videos. But this is usually because either YouTube doesn't know about it or hasn't discovered any violations yet, or because there is some legal gray area included.

- **Better Safe than Sorry:** Just remember that in order to be safe and avoid headaches down the road, just buy the necessary licenses for what you use in your videos. This can damage your reputation and channel if you don't take these precautions and play it safe while you can.

- **Manual or Automatic Penalties:** Violating any copyrights can lead to either a manual or automatic YouTube penalty. In either case, it's hard to get rid of this type of violation or remove the record of it. Even worse than that, you will have a hard time monetizing your content down the road. If you did violate these rules, your account won't be allowed to be monetized again in the future.

The Analytics of YouTube:

For users of YouTube who are more experienced, but new to monetizing, perhaps you have noticed a new area of information in the analytics suite area on the site. This covers the estimated and existing earnings suite. Using that, you can visualize the trends of both your past and current trends, along with an estimation of future earnings according to your current trends and performance. Having this information will give you a huge leg up, and staying on top of how well your videos are doing is a must. Remember that the reports for estimated earnings on YouTube are only visible when you have your account on AdSense already linked.

Thresholds of Payment:

When you earn on YouTube, you have to give your personal tax info as soon as you can get payments. This means anything above 10 dollars. As soon as you've earned that much, you have to verify any information of yours for YouTube, along with your phone number and address.

Asking for Donations:

A more direct way to earn through YouTube is to simply ask for donations. This can be done either directly on your videos, or by linking a "Go Fund Me" account to your YouTube by entering the link into your video descriptions. Some people will have success with this, while others won't. Only you can decide whether that method is right for you.

Chapter 6
More Tips for Earning and Creating Traffic

Although we've covered a lot of good content and methods for creating income using YouTube, there are some other solutions you can use to create revenue through this platform. Rather than seeing YouTube itself as a way to monetize on its own, try to view it as a useful catalyst you can utilize. It's most valuable as a network, and not as the end product itself.

Alternative Earning Methods on YouTube:

- **Using Shopify:** We've already told you that YouTube is in second place for the place of the largest search engine on earth. When thinking of marketing, it would be foolish to ignore this huge resource you have available to you for free. But how can you take advantage of this? When it comes to physical products, Shopify is a good website to use for your e-commerce store, which you will then link to from YouTube.

- **Seeing Videos using Yondo:** When you have a goal of earning money from just your video content itself and not by using the videos to redirect people to buy physical products, there is a better choice than just hoping for high ad revenue. Make a channel, get a following, build your business brand, and then start directing your video audience to landing pages that will set them up with premium content and videos. One good way to do that is Yondo, which allows you to make a personal store for selling videos using your domain. This gives you the choice to sell monthly subscriptions and rentals that go on pay per view. But the best part is that you can set your own price and won't need to split your revenue with YouTube.

- **Using Sponsorships:** When you look at YouTube creators who are the most successful, you will soon see that there are sponsorships and ads on or in their videos. Typically, these represent opportunities the creators have found by themselves. The best thing about using these sponsorships is that the money you earn is all your own, and YouTube doesn't get a big cut of it. In addition to this, you will be able to negotiate the contracts that you wish to negotiate as needed according to your audience size. Usually, the number of revenue you get from these sponsorships adds up to more than you'd earn from just ad revenue.

  Of course, this doesn't mean you shouldn't try to benefit from both! Then you will have a couple of different income streams from just one source, and what could be better than that?

- **Think about Live Speaking Eventually:** Another way to increase your reputation on YouTube is to attract engagements for live speaking to your channel. If the channel you are producing on YouTube has a specific audience or niche, conduct some online research about any conferences or events that are happening and need speakers. You can then use your statistics on YouTube, along with your top clips, then pitch yourself to the people directing the events in need of speakers. Being involved in these types of engagements is a great way to earn money. In fact, you can earn up to thousands with just a presentation lasting a single hour. Don't miss out on this chance and always look for different ways to make your audience grow.

Think Creatively to Earn a YouTube Income:

Are you able to earn real income using YouTube? Of course you are. Will you do this by only relying on ad revenue based on audience impressions? That isn't as likely. Rather, you should identify methods that you can use to leverage the gigantic network on YouTube to bring streams of revenue in and earn a massive passive income. You might try to do this and find that you aren't receiving as many likes, subscribers, or views as you want. That's because there is no shortage of competition on YouTube, with all of the creators and viewers on the site. You might now be asking how you can make your content gain exposure and stand out in the crowd. Here are some tips you can use to do that.

- **Do Video Transcriptions:** One way to make your videos more successful and attractive to viewers is to transcribe the content in the video and post it inside of the description of your video. Websites are not yet able to fetch keywords accurately from the audio spoken in video content, so at this time, written words are a big factor for the rankings of videos. If you already have a good presentation within your video, use speechpad.com or other similar resources to transcribe the words and get plenty of SEO boost for your ranks. Then paste this into the description field of your video. That makes your video simpler to absorb and consume and will lead to a boost in your rankings along the way.

- **Make a Video Reply:** YouTube lets you post comments as a video reply when it comes to some videos, meaning that videos you do publish allow others to leave you a response as a video comment. This will then reference your content and show underneath your video. This also works the opposite way, too. You can look up a video with a lot of views and leave your personal video as a comment response. This will lead millions to see your content, simply because you did this. But remember that this can only be done one time, so make your choice carefully and wisely. For example, if you are posting videos about apps for Android, find the most popular video about this and post yours as a video reply.

- **Make sure you Direct Links to your Content:** The majority of people view outside SEO as a method for boosting existing rankings for their personal domain pages. However, this also can matter a lot in your YouTube video's rankings. When you can get plenty of high sources or authority blogs to direct people to your videos, they will gain a higher keyword ranking and get more visitors. From your personal page, viewers will see more details on your video content which will then heighten the rankings there, too. This will eventually lead to a popular video network feeding huge amounts of traffic to each other and constantly getting bigger and bigger.

In order to save yourself some time working with external SEO, visit a site like AudienceBloom.com and use their service to your advantage. But there is another trick for this. When you use your blog to embed your video content, underneath the video you can add another link that leads back to the video. Make sure that you enter information about what the video is about here. This then improves the SEO juice your content has. The majority if videos on YouTube will not have other links pointing back to them, so this trick will help you go far.

- **Inserting other Videos:** Okay, so now you have put in a lot of hard work to get others to watch your content and videos. This is a great chance to show related content as the very end of your existing videos. If people have watched your video all the way to the end, this is the time when they are the most interested and engaged with it. If, with each video you create, you add links to your other content, you will have a big network of videos that interlink to each other, adding to your traffic and overall rankings. It would be a shame to miss out on this opportunity.

As you can see, there is a theme that recurs in these simple tips and tricks. They are easy and simple to apply to everything you create. What that means is that you are able to use this no matter what type of video you have to create more comments, subscribers, likes, and views overall. And since you are also linking to related videos, your empire of videos will grow and grow, leading to plenty of visitors and interested leads to your brand and site each day. This is how you earn money using YouTube.

Conclusion

Thank for making it through to the end of *YouTube: The Secret to Building an Audience and Creating a Massive Passive Income*. Let's hope it was informative and able to provide you with all of the tools you need to achieve your goals of earning money using YouTube. Since YouTube is the biggest video platform on the internet today, it would be a shame to waste the potential it provides you for earning a passive income.

The next step is to create engaging, quality content that focuses on being helpful and giving, getting a quality video setup, and driving traffic to your YouTube page. This will then allow viewers to see a link to your store. You can also try asking for donations or using ads, as described in the book.

Finally, if you found this book useful in any way, a review on Amazon is always appreciated!

Check Out My Other Books

Below you'll find some of my other popular books that are popular on Amazon and Kindle as well. Simply go to the links below to check them out.

https://www.amazon.com/Facebook-Marketing-Building-Growing-Business/dp/1544865864/

https://www.amazon.com/Penny-Stocks-Achieve-Financial-Freedom/dp/1544092199/

https://www.amazon.com/Passive-Income-Quit-Your-Terms/dp/1541338731/

https://www.amazon.com/Dividend-Investing-investors-creating-financial/dp/1542926815/

https://www.amazon.com/Affiliate-Marketing-Creating-Massive-Business/dp/1542477549/

https://www.amazon.com/Network-Marketing-Building-Successful-Affiliate/dp/1542532671/

Description

Who doesn't dream of building a financially independent life for themselves and being their own boss? In our modern day, this is more possible than it's ever been in the past. In *YouTube: The Secret to Building an Audience and Creating a Massive Passive Income*, you will be learning about using YouTube to do this. In its chapters, you will find out:

- **How to Make Engaging Videos:** What actual equipment do you need for making quality videos? Is there anything you need to purchase, or do you already have the correct tools? Find out in chapter one. You will also learn about the right attitude to have for making videos that bring in more traffic.

- **How to Grow your Traffic:** Making YouTube videos is the easy part, but how do you get people to actually want to watch them? And after you get their attention, how do you get them to stay and subscribe? There is a lot to this process which you will find out about in this book.

- **Using AdSense and Selling:** Selling products on YouTube can be difficult if you don't know where to start. There are a few different options for this, including selling digital and physical products, by using links or advertising products on

YouTube. You will find out more about this in chapters four, five, and six of this guide.

Earning an income from home doesn't have to be rocket science or even difficult. All it takes is a willingness to learn, enthusiasm for what you're doing, and a desire to add value to your viewer's lives.